# 221

# WAYS TO SUCCESS

## TIMELESS QUOTES OF GREAT MASTERS FOR A FULFILLED LIFE

# N. RAMAN

INDIA · SINGAPORE · MALAYSIA

# Notion Press Media Pvt Ltd

No. 50, Chettiyar Agaram Main Road,
Vanagaram, Chennai, Tamil Nadu – 600 095

First Published by Notion Press 2021
Copyright © N. Raman 2021
All Rights Reserved.

ISBN 979-8-88521-458-2

# *Preface*

Humanity is at crossroads. Technology disruptions in personal, social, cultural and professional lives of people have take a heavy toll on the basic fabric of ideal living. Environmental destruction coupled with ever increasing greed and rat race have left human race in an unenviable position. Added to this is the Global Pandemic that has thrown life out of gear. People have moved away from the eternal values that our ancestors have been advocating for centuries. Values such as gratitude, forgiveness, inner happiness, self-evolution, unselfishness, lack of ego and such other pure emotions are dwindling fast.

This book is an honest attempt to address these lacunae by drawing the attention of people at large to the basic values of good, peaceful and prosperous living as a well-knit Global community. The ultimate objective is to reach masses with these gems by translating the book in several languages.

The inspiration that formed the foundation of this books has come from:

- The enormous positive effect that short poems of Thirukkural (Tamil literature) have had on humanity for centuries, and

- Urgent need for people to access collection of noble thoughts of some of the great people – all in one place.

Readers can take three or four quotes from this book every week and apply them in their day to day activities. In this way, over a period of 12 months, one can transform his or her life fully by following these precious gems. These quotations are short, simple and easy to understand. Nevertheless, it requires concerted efforts to apply them consistently in our lives.

Finally, our Humble Prostrations to all our Gurus for the ancient wisdom that they have left behind for generations to benefit.

# 221 Ways to Success

1.  *"For a seed to achieve its greatest expression, it must come completely undone. The shell cracks, the insides come out and everything changes. To someone who does not understand personal growth, it would look like complete destruction."*

    **– Cynthia Occelli**

2.  *"It is not the answer that enlightens, but the question."*

    **– Eugene Ionesco**

3.  *"The way to find out about happiness is to keep your mind on those moments when you feel most happy – not excited, not just thrilled, but deeply happy. This requires a little bit of self-analysis. What is it that makes you happy? Stay with it, no matter what people tell you. This is what is called following your bliss."*

    **– Joseph Campbell**

4. *"It does not matter how slowly you go as long as you do not stop."*

**– Confucius**

5. *"Don't judge each day by the harvest you reap, but by the seeds you plant."*

**– Robert Louis Stevenson**

6. *"I slept and dreamt that life was a joy. I awoke and saw that life was service. I acted and behold, service was joy."*

**– Rabindranath Tagore**

7. *"A man can be himself only so long as he is alone; and if he does not love solitude, he will not love freedom; for it is only when he is alone that he is really free."*

**– Arthur Schopenhauer**

8. *"Wise men speak because they have something to say; fools because they have to say something."*

**– Plato**

9. *"Anything which is more than our necessity is poison. It may be power, wealth, hunger, ego, greed, laziness, love, ambition, hate or anything."*

**– Rumi**

10. *"No one is born hating another person because of the color of his skin or his background or his religion."*

**– Nelson Mandela**

11. *"We choose our joys and sorrows long before we experience them."*

**– Khalil Gibran**

12. *"Once you feel you are avoided by someone, never disturb them again."*

**– Buddha**

13. *"The key to growth is to the introduction of consciousness into our awareness."*

**– Lao Tzu**

14.  *"Happiness is when what you think and what you do are in harmony."*

    **– Mahatma Gandhi**

15.  *"Our past is a story existing only in our minds. Look, analyze, understand and forgive. Then, as quickly as possible, chuck it."*

    **– Marianne Williamson**

16.  *"The work always leaves you with less of a story. Who would you be without your story? You never know until you inquire. There is no story that is you or that leads to you. Every story leads away from you. Turn it around; undo it. You are what exists before all stories. You are what remains when the story is understood."*

    **– Byron Katie**

17.  *"If you shut the door to all errors, truth will be shut."*

    **– Rabindranath Tagore**

18. *"Only from the Heart can you touch the sky."*

**– Rumi**

19. *"Talent hits a target no one else can hit. Genius hits a target no one else can see."*

**– Arthur Schopenhauer**

20. *"Without your wounds where would your power be? Very angels themselves cannot persuade the wretched and blundering children on earth as can one human being broken on the wheels of living. In love's service only wounded soldiers can serve."*

**– Thornton Wilder**

21. *"I walked out of the door toward the gate that would lead to my freedom. I knew, if I didn't leave my bitterness and hatred behind, I would still be in prison."*

**– Nelson Mandela**

22. *"When I hear somebody sigh, "Life is hard", I am always tempted to ask, "compared to what?""*

**– Sydney J. Harris**

23. *"Life has no meaning. Each of us has meaning and we bring it to life. It is a waste to be asking the question when you are the answer."*

**– Joseph Campbell**

24. *"Everyone is still healing from things they don't talk about, so be KIND."*

**– Buddha**

25. *"Numbing the pain for a while will make it worse when you finally feel it."*

**– Professor Albus Dumbledore**

26. *"We all need to look into the dark side of the nature – that is where the energy is, the passion. People are afraid of that because it holds pieces of us we 've been busy denying."*

    **– Sue Grafton**

27. *"There is no sincere love than the love of food."*

    **– George Bernard Shaw**

28. *"Life is an art of drawing without an eraser."*

    **– John W. Gardner**

29. *"You may forget with whom you laughed, but you will never forget with whom you wept."*

    **– Khalil Gibran**

30. *"Death is not extinguishing the light; it is only putting out the lamp because the dawn has come."*

    **– Rabindranath Tagore**

31. *"Never discourage anyone who continually makes progress, no matter how slow."*

**– Plato**

32. *"We wait all these years to find someone who understands us, I thought, someone who accepts us as we are, someone with a wizard's power to melt stone to sunlight, who can bring us happiness in spite of trials, who can face our dragons in the night, who can transform us into the soul we choose to be. Just yesterday I found that magical someone is the face we see in the mirror; it is us and underneath our home- made masks."*

**– Richard Bach**

33. *"Surviving is important, thriving is elegant."*

**– Maya Angelou**

34. *"The attempt to escape from pain is what creates more pain."*

**– Gabor Mate**

35. *"The most beautiful people we have known are those who have known defeat, known suffering, known struggle, known loss, and have found their way out of the depths. These people have an appreciation, a sensitivity, and an understanding of life that fills them with compassion, gentleness, and a deep loving concern. Beautiful people do not just happen."*

**– Dr. Elisabeth Kubler-Ross**

36. *"Abundance is a process of letting go; that which is empty can receive."*

**– Bryant H. McGill**

37. *"It was not the feeling of completeness I so needed, but the feeling of not being empty."*

**– Jonathan Safran Foer**

38. *"If a man is to live, he must be all alive, body, soul, mind, heart, spirit."*

**– Thomas Merton**

39. *"The main interest of my work is not concerned with the treatment of neuroses but rather with the approach to the numinous. But the fact that the approach to the numinous is the real therapy, and in as much as you attain to the numinous experience you are released from the curse of pathology."*

**– Carl Jung**

40. *"Resentment is like drinking poison and hoping it will kill your enemies."*

**– Nelson Mandela**

41. *"Mostly it is loss which teaches us about the worth of things."*

**– Arthur Schopenhauer**

42. *"A deep sense of love and belonging is an irreducible need of all people. We are biologically, cognitively, physically, and spiritually wired to love, to be loved, and to belong. When those needs are not met, we don't function as we were meant to. We break. We fall apart. We numb. We ache. We hurt others. We get sick."*

**– Brene Brown**

43. *"Life is an Echo. What you send out comes back. What you sow, you reap. What you give you get. What you see in others exists in you."*

**– Buddha**

44. *"Stay close to anything that makes you glad you are alive."*

**– Hafez**

45. *"Listen to the Music of the soul with the chords of your heart attuned, with the strings of your thoughts in unison, with the divine musician."*

**– Swami Jyothir Maya Nanda**

46. *"The divine is not something high above us. It is in heaven, it is in earth, it is inside us."*

**— Morihei Ueshiba**

47. *"The appearance of things changes according to the emotions; and thus, we see magic and beauty in them, while the magic and beauty are really in ourselves."*

**— Khalil Gibran**

48. *"Gratitude, the ability to count your blessings, is the ultimate way to connect with the heart."*

**— Baptist De Pape**

49. *"Let the beauty we love be what we do. There are hundreds of ways to kneel and kiss the ground."*

**— Rumi**

50. *"Act in earnest and you will become earnest in all you do."*

**— William James**

51. *"It always seems impossible until it is done."*

   **– Nelson Mandela**

52. *"Money is the worst discovery of human life. But it is the most trusted material to test human nature."*

   **– Buddha**

53. *"Let us not pray to be sheltered from dangers but to be fearless when facing them."*

   **– Rabindranath Tagore**

54. *"A hundred times I remind myself that my inner and outer life are based on the labors of other men, living and dead, and that I must exert myself in order to give in the same measure as I have received and am still receiving."*

   **– Albert Einstein**

55. *"Progress is impossible without change, and those who cannot change their minds cannot change anything."*

   **– George Bernard Shaw**

56. *"Good people do not need laws to tell them to act responsibly, while bad people will find a way around the laws."*

**– Plato**

57. *"Trust in dreams, for in them is the hidden gate of eternity."*

**– Khalil Gibran**

58. *"Excellence is doing ordinary things extraordinarily well."*

**– John W. Gardner**

59. *"Education is not the learning of facts but the training of the mind to think."*

**– Albert Einstein**

60. *"Our prayers should be for blessings in general, for God knows best what is good for us."*

**– Socrates**

61. *"A flower cannot blossom without sunshine, and man cannot live without love."*

    **– Max Muller**

62. *"The bad news: Nothing is permanent. The good news: Nothing is permanent."*

    **– Lolly Daskal**

63. *"To begin, begin."*

    **– William Wordsworth**

64. *"Every man takes the limits of his own field of vision for the limits of the world."*

    **– Arthur Schopenhauer**

65. *"The greatest enemy of knowledge is not ignorance; it is the illusion of knowledge."*

    **– Stephen Hawking**

**21**

66. *"One day you'll just be a memory for some people. Do your best to be a good one."*

          **– Buddha**

67. *"Non acceptance of uncertainty is Fear. If we accept that uncertainty it becomes Adventure."*

          **– Rumi**

68. *"Non acceptance of good in others is Envy. If we accept that Good, it becomes inspiration."*

          **– Rumi**

69. *"Non acceptance of things which are beyond our control is Anger. If we accept, it becomes tolerance"*

          **– Rumi**

70. *"Non acceptance of Person as he is, is Hatred. If we accept Person unconditionally, it becomes Love."*

          **– Rumi**

71. *"If you suffer, it is because of you. If you feel blissful, it is because of you. Nobody else is responsible. Only you and you alone. You are your hell and heaven too."*

**– Osho**

72. *"No matter how hard the past, you can always begin again."*

**– Buddha**

73. *"You never know what is enough unless you know what is more than enough."*

**– William Blake**

74. *"It is not enough we do our best, sometimes we must do what is required."*

**– Winston S. Churchill**

75. *"Sometimes people don't want to hear the truth because they don't want their illusions destroyed."*

**– Friedrich Nietzsche**

76. *"Happiness in intelligent people is the rarest thing I know."*

**– Ernest Hemingway**

77. *"An idiot with a plan can beat a genius without a plan."*

**– Warren Buffett**

78. *"When life itself seems lunatic, who knows where madness lies? Perhaps to be too practical is madness. To surrender dreams – this may be madness. Too much sanity may be madness – and maddest of all: to see life as it is, and not as it should be!."*

**– Don Quixote**

79. *"The highest education is that which does not merely give us information but makes our life in harmony with all existence."*

**– Rabindranath Tagore**

80. *"The goal of meditation isn't to control your thoughts, it's to stop letting them control you."*

**– Buddha**

81. *"A life spent making mistakes is not only more honorable, but more useful than a life spent doing nothing."*

**– George Bernard Shaw**

82. *"The greatest glory in living lies not in never falling, but in rising every time we fall."*

**– Nelson Mandela**

83. *"The secret of happiness, you see is not found in seeking more. But in capacity to enjoy less."*

**– Socrates**

84. *"The greatest Happiness is to know the source of Unhappiness."*

**– Fyodor Dosteovsky**

85. *"History never looks like history when you are living through it."*

**– John W. Gardner**

86. *"We are what we think. All that we are, arises with our thoughts. With our thoughts, we make the world."*

**– Buddha**

87. *"Equanimity is about finding a way to be ok even when nothing else is, allowing us to experience peace in stressful situations. In the midst of movement and chaos, keep stillness inside you."*

**– D. Chopra**

88. *"Stop trying to calm the storm. Calm yourself, the storm will pass."*

**– Buddha**

89. *"Wisdom is the reward you get for a life-time of listening when you rather would have talked."*

— **Mark Twain**

90. *"Feel the feeling but don't become the emotion. Witness it. Allow it. Release it."*

— **Crystal Andrus**

91. *"New friends may be poems, but old friends are alphabets. Do not forget the alphabets because you will need them to read the poems."*

— **Shakespeare**

92. *"Poetry is the spontaneous overflow of powerful feelings; it takes its origin from emotion recollected in tranquility."*

— **William Wordsworth**

93. *"The high- minded man must care more for the Truth than for what people think."*

— **Aristotle**

94.  "There is a fundamental distinction between strategy and operational effectiveness."

**– Michael Porter**

95.  "How mankind defers from day to day the best it can do, and the most beautiful things it can enjoy, without thinking that every day may be the last one, and that lost time is lost eternity."

**– Max muller**

96.  "Being both soft and strong is a combination very few have mastered."

**– Yasmin Mogahed**

97.  "We seldom think of what we have, but always of what we lack."

**– Arthur Schopenhauer**

98.  "If you are looking for friend who is faultless, you'll be friendless."

**– Rumi**

99. *"It is very simple to be Happy, but it is very difficult to be simple."*

**– Rabindranath Tagore**

100. *"It is not enough to dream, you must act. Without action, a door is just a wall."*

**– J M Storm**

101. *"No amount of anxiety makes any difference to anything that is going to happen."*

**– Alan Watts**

102. *"Do not judge by appearances; a rich heart may be under a poor coat."*

**– Scottish Proverb**

103. *"When something is gone, something better is coming."*

**– Dalai Lama**

104. *"Excellence is not a gift, but a skill that takes practice. We do not act rightly because we are excellent, in fact we achieve excellence by acting rightly."*

   **– Plato**

105. *"Two things you will never have to chase: True friends and true love."*

   **– Buddha**

106. *"When you arise in the morning, think of what a precious privilege it is to be alive to breathe, to think, to enjoy, to love."*

   **– Marcus Aurelius**

107. *"Lose an hour in the morning, and you will spend all day looking for it."*

   **– Richard Whately**

108. *"Your living is determined not so much by what life brings to you as by the attitude you bring to life; not so much by what happens to you as by the way your mind looks at what happens."*

**– Khalil Gibran**

109. *"Compassion is the basis of morality."*

**– Arthur Schopenhauer**

110. *"Few are those who see with their own eyes and feel with their own hearts."*

**– Albert Einstein**

111. *"Be kind to all creatures. This is the TRUE Religion."*

**– Buddha**

112. *"True happiness involves the full use of one's power and talents."*

**–John W. Gardner**

113. *"I attribute my success to this — I never gave or took any excuse. "*

   **– Florence Nightingale**

114. *"I think one's feelings waste themselves in words; they ought to be distilled into actions which bring results."*

   **– Florence Nightingale**

115. *"Faith is the bird that feels the light when the dawn is still dark."*

   **– Rabindranath Tagore**

116. *"Human behavior flows from three main sources: desire, emotion, and knowledge."*

   **– Plato**

117. *"It is difficult to find happiness within oneself, but it is impossible to find it anywhere else."*

   **–Arthur Schopenhauer**

118.    *"Fake friends are like shadows. They follow you in Sun but leave you in Dark."*

**– Buddha**

119.    *"What we need is not the will to believe, but the wish to find out."*

**– William Wordsworth**

120.    *"He who reigns within himself and rules passions, desires and fears is more than a king."*

**– John Milton**

121.    *"It is easier to forgive an enemy than to forgive a friend."*

**– William Blake**

122.    *"Choose to be optimistic. It feels better."*

**– Dalai Lama**

123.   *"The only true wisdom is in knowing you know nothing."*

**— Socrates**

124.   *"That is the returning to God which in reality is never concluded on earth but yet leaves behind in the soul a divine homesickness, which never again ceases."*

**— Max Muller**

125.   *"We forfeit three-fourths of ourselves in order to be like other people."*

**— Arthur Schopenhauer**

126.   *"Don't be a beggar of love, be a donor of love. Beautiful people are not always good. But good people are always beautiful."*

**— Buddha**

127.   *"The essence of strategy is choosing what not to do."*

**— Michael Porter**

128. *"We are all faced with a series of great opportunities — brilliantly disguised as insoluble problems."*

**— John W. Gardner**

129. *"Not failure, but low aim is sin."*

**— Benjamin E. Mays**

130. *"The butterfly counts not months but moments and has time enough."*

**— Rabindranath Tagore**

131. *"Democracy is a device that ensures we shall be governed no better than we deserve."*

**— George Bernard Shaw**

132. *"You pray in your distress and in your need; would that you might pray also in the fullness of your joy and in your days of abundance."*

**— Khalil Gibran**

133.  *"The best portion of a man's life is his little, nameless, unremembered acts of kindness and love."*

**– William Wordsworth**

134.  *"The secret of change is to focus all of your energy not on fighting the old, but on building the new."*

**– Socrates**

135.  *"The single biggest problem in communication is the illusion that it has taken place."*

**– George Bernard Shaw**

136.  *"Men talk of killing time, while time quietly kills them."*

**– Dion Boucicault**

137.  *"Necessity, the mother of invention."*

**– George Farquhar**

138.   *"When the blind lead the blind, no wonder they both fall into matrimony."*

**– George Farquhar**

139.   *"My life is every moment of my life. It is not the culmination of the past."*

**– Hugh Leonard**

140.   *"Good actions give strength to ourselves and inspire good actions in others."*

**– Plato**

141.   *"Look deep into the nature, and then you will understand everything better."*

**– Albert Einstein**

142.   *"Spend your time on those that love you unconditionally. Don't waste it on those that only love you when the conditions are right for them."*

**– Buddha**

143.   *"Innovation is the central issue in economic prosperity."*

**– Michael Porter**

144.   *"A man should look for what is, and not for what he thinks should be."*

**– Albert Einstein**

145.   *"Gratitude is born of humility, for it acknowledges giftedness of the creation and the benevolence of the Creator. This recognition gives birth to acts marked by attention and responsibility. Ingratitude on the other hand is marked by hubris, which denies the gift, and this always leads to inattention, irresponsibility, and abuse."*

**– Mark T. Mitchell**

146.   *"You got to look for the good in the bad, the happy in your sad, the gain in your pain, and what makes you grateful and not hateful."*

**– Karen Salmansohn**

147. *"A hunch is creativity trying to tell you something."*

— **Frank Capra**

148. *"Intuition is seeing with the soul."*

— **Dean Koontz**

149. *"A sense of humor is the only divine quality of man."*

— **Arthur Schopenhauer**

150. *"It's hard to like some one you don't trust, and it is hard to like yourself if you don't trust yourself."*

— **Leo Babauta**

151. *"Your intuition knows what to do. The trick is getting head to shut up so you can hear."*

— **Louise Smith**

152.  *"One can have no smaller or greater mastering than mastering of oneself."*

— **Leonardo Da Vinci**

153.  *"No human relation gives one possession in another — every two souls are absolutely different. In friendship or in love, the two side by side raise hands together to find what one cannot reach alone."*

— **Khalil Gibran**

154.  *"Everything comes to us that belongs to us if we create the capacity to receive it."*

— **Rabindranath Tagore**

155.  *"It must be borne in mind that the tragedy of life doesn't lie in not reaching your goal. The tragedy lies in having no goals to reach."*

— **Benjamin E. Mays**

156. *"A painful Truth is always better than a hidden lie."*

**– Buddha**

157. *"We don't stop playing because we grow old; we grow old because we stop playing."*

**– George Bernard Shaw**

158. *"A good head and a good heart are always a formidable combination. But when you add to that a literate tongue or pen, then you have something very special."*

**– Nelson Mandela**

159. *"Imagination is more important than knowledge. Knowledge is limited. Imagination encircles the world."*

**– Albert Einstein**

160. *"If you don't like something, change it. If you can't change it, change your attitude."*

**– Maya Angelou**

161. *"Mistakes are painful when they happen, but years later a collection of mistakes called experience which leads us to success."*

   **– A.P.J. Abdul Kalam**

162. *"The greatest gift you can give someone is your time, because when you give your time you are giving a portion of your life that you will never get back."*

   **– Buddha**

163. *"Life doesn't get easier or more forgiving, we get stronger and more resilient."*

   **– Steve Maraboli**

164. *"Be kind. Everyone you meet is fighting a great battle."*

   **– Philo of Alexandria**

165. *"The greatest weapon against stress is our ability to choose one thought over another."*

   **– William James**

166. *"You have been criticizing yourself for years and it hasn't worked. Try approving of yourself and see what happens."*

**– Louise L. Hay**

167. *"It's surprising how many persons go through life without ever recognizing that their feelings towards other people are largely determined by their feelings towards themselves, and if you are not comfortable within yourself, you can't be comfortable with others."*

**– Sydney J. Harris**

168. *"People who learn to control inner experience will be able to determine the quality of their lives, which is as close as any of us can come to being happy."*

**– Mihaly Csikszentmihalyi**

169. *"Knowing yourself is the beginning of all wisdom."*

**– Aristotle**

170.   *"Nothing in life is to be feared, it is only to be understood. Now is the time to understand more so that we may fear less."*

*– Marie Curie*

171.   *"Never feel sad about losing anything in life, because whenever a tree loses a leaf a new leaf grows in its place."*

*– A.P.J. Abdul Kalam*

172.   *"Courage is not the absence of fear, but rather the judgement that something else is more important than fear."*

*– Ambrose Redmoon*

173.   *"Complaining does not work as a strategy. We all have finite time and energy. Any time we spend in whining is unlikely to help us achieve our goals, and it won't make us happier."*

*– Randy Pausch*

174.  *"A beautiful face means nothing when the heart is ugly."*

**– Buddha**

175.  *"We will gradually become indifferent to what goes on in the minds of other people when we acquire a knowledge of the superficial nature of their thoughts, the narrowness of their views and of the number of their errors. Whoever attaches a lot of value to the opinions of others pays them too much honor."*

**– Arthur Schopenhauer**

176.  *"You give but little when you give of your possessions. It is when you give of yourself, you truly give."*

**– Khalil Gibran**

177.  *"A brave man is not the one who does not feel afraid, but he who conquers that fear."*

**– Nelson Mandela**

178.  "*Being true to your emotions can't help but make you feel better about yourself, for you are able to be authentic.*"

**– Dr. Goldsmith**

179.  "*Think good thoughts, say nice things, do good for others. Everything comes back.*"

**– Buddha**

180.  "*Faith is a knowledge within the heart beyond the reach of proof.*"

**– Khalil Gibran**

181.  "*Let the beauty of what you love, be what you do.*"

**– Rumi**

182.  "*When a deep injury is done to us, we never heal until we forgive.*"

**– Nelson Mandela**

183. *"The present moment is filled with joy and happiness. If you are attentive, you will see it."*

**– Thich Nhat Hanh**

184. *"Radical acceptance rests on letting go of the illusion of control and a willingness to notice and accept things as they are right now, without judging. We choose to wholeheartedly accept what has happened to us at the depths of our minds, bodies and souls. We feel a lightening, a release, and a sense of peace."*

**– Marsha Linehan**

185. *"When you hold resentment towards another, you are bound to that person or condition by an emotional link that is stronger than steel. Forgiveness is the only way to dissolve that link and get free."*

**– Catherine Ponder**

186. *"The weak can never forgive. Forgiveness is the attribute of the strong."*

**– Mahatma Gandhi**

187. *"Bring acceptance into your non acceptance. Bring surrender into your non surrender. Then see what happens."*

**— Eckhart Tolle**

188. *"A successful man is one who can lay a firm foundation with the bricks others have thrown at him."*

**— David Brinkley**

189. *"Find the place inside where there is joy, and the joy will burn out the pain."*

**— Joseph Campbell**

190. *"There are only two ways to live your life. One is as though nothing is a miracle. The other is as though everything is a miracle."*

**— Albert Einstein**

191. *"Through love all pain will turn to medicine."*

**— Rumi**

192. *"Your children are not your children. They are the sons and daughters of life's longing for itself."*

**– Khalil Gibran**

193. *"False words are not only evil in themselves, but they infect the soul with evil."*

**– Plato**

194. *"Forgiveness liberates the soul that is why it is such a powerful weapon."*

**– Nelson Mandela**

195. *"The best thing you can ever do is to believe in yourself."*

**– Buddha**

196. *"Comfort zones are where dreams go to die."*

**– Lisa Cypers Kamen**

197.   *"Time does not change us. It just unfolds us."*

**– Max Frisch**

198.   *"Good leaders need positive agenda, not just agenda of dealing with crisis."*

**– Michael Porter**

199.   *"Spread love wherever you go. Let no one ever come to you without leaving happier."*

**– Mother Teresa**

200.   *"Never waste your time trying to explain who you are to people who are committed to misunderstanding you."*

**– Shannon L. Alder**

201.   *"Experience is the hardest kind of teacher. It gives you the test first and the lesson afterward."*

**– Oscar Wilde**

202. *"It's easy to judge. It's more difficult to understand. Understanding requires compassion, patience, and a willingness to believe that good hearts sometimes choose poor methods. Through judging, we separate. Through understanding, we grow."*

**– Doe Zantamata**

203. *"Thinking is difficult, that's why most people judge."*

**– Carl Jung**

204. *"I am not "HANDSOME." But I can give my "HAND" to "SOME", one who need help. Beauty is in Heart, not on face."*

**– Swami Vivekananda**

205. *"Small changes can make a big difference."*

**– Buddha**

206. *"You have to dream before your dreams can come true."*

**– A.P.J. Abdul Kalam**

207. *"Successful and unsuccessful people do not vary greatly in their abilities. They vary in their desires to reach their potential."*

   *– John Maxwell*

208. *"So, the problem is not so much to see what nobody has yet seen, as to think what nobody has yet thought concerning that which everybody sees."*

   *– Arthur Schopenhauer*

209. *"The best brains of the nation may be found on the last benches of the classroom."*

   *– A.P.J. Abdul Kalam*

210. *"Try not to become a man of success, but rather try to become a man of value."*

   *– Albert Einstein*

211. *"Lead from the back. Let others believe they are in front."*

   *– Nelson Mandela*

212. *"To belittle, you have to be little."*

**– Khalil Gibran**

213. *"We are what our thoughts have made us; so, take care about what you think. Words are secondary. Thoughts live; They travel far."*

**– Swami Vivekananda**

214. *"I am not a product of my circumstances. I am a product of my decisions."*

**– Stephen R. Covey**

215. *"Don't make permanent decisions based on temporary feelings."*

**– Bobby Umar**

216. *"Most people live – whether physically, intellectually or morally – in a very restricted circle of their potential being. We all have reservoirs of life to draw upon of which we do not dream."*

**– William James**

217. *"Trust yourself. Create the kind of life you will be happy to live with all your life. Make the most of yourself by fanning the tiny, inner sparks of possibility into flames of achievement."*

   **– Foster C. McClellan**

218. *"Life is no brief candle for me. It is a sort of splendid torch which I have got hold of for the moment, and I want to make it burn as brightly as possible before handing it on to future generations."*

   **– George Bernard Shaw**

219. *"Sure, I am that this day we are masters of our fate, that the task which has been set before us is not above our strengths; that its pangs and toils are not beyond my endurance. As long as we have faith in our own cause and an unconquerable will to win, victory will not be denied to us."*

   **– Winston Churchill**

220. *"A moment of patience in a moment of anger saves you a hundred moments of regret."*

**– Buddha**

221. *"When I admire the wonder of a sunset or the beauty of the moon, my soul expands in worship of the Creator."*

**– Mahatma Gandhi**

Made in the USA
Las Vegas, NV
17 January 2023

65762812R00035